The Ancient Olympic Games

ILLUSTRATED BY JHONNY NÚÑEZ

Published in paperback in Great Britain in 2020 by Wayland
Text © Hodder and Stoughton, 2019
Illustrations © Jhonny Núñez

All rights reserved.

Editors: Sarah Ridley and Paul Rockett
Designer: Lisa Peacock

Wayland, an imprint of Hachette Children's Group
Part of Hodder & Stoughton
Carmelite House
50 Victoria Embankment
London EC4Y 0DZ
ISBN: 978 1 5263 1010 1

Printed and bound in China

MIX
Paper | Supporting responsible forestry
FSC® C104740

An Hachette UK Company
www.hachette.co.uk
www.hachettechildrens.co.uk

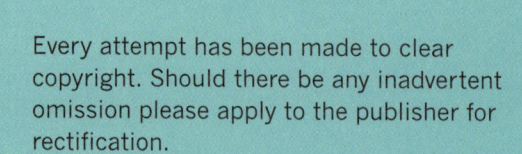

Every attempt has been made to clear copyright. Should there be any inadvertent omission please apply to the publisher for rectification.

Picture credits:
44t: elgreko/Shutterstock; 44b: Eye Ubiquitous/Alamy; 45tl: Archive World/Alamy; 45tr: Kyodo News/Newscom/Alamy; 45b: Rodolfo Buhr/La Imagem/Fotoarena/Alamy.

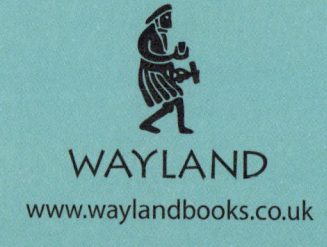

WAYLAND
www.waylandbooks.co.uk

CONTENTS

The Olympic Festival	4	The Javelin	26
A Legendary Beginning	6	Wrestling	28
The Glory of Zeus	8	Boxing	30
The Olympic Site	10	The Pankration	32
Training	12	Race in Armour	34
The Spectators and Judges	14	Chariot Races	36
The First Race	16	Heralds and Trumpeters	38
Triastes	18	The Women's Games	40
The Pentathlon	20	Hail the Champions	42
The Discus	22	The Olympic Legacy	44
The Long Jump	24		
		Further Information	46
		Glossary	47
		Index	48

The Olympic Festival

Every fourth year, from 776 BCE to CE 393, citizens from all over the Greek world flocked to Olympia, on the west coast of the Peloponnese in Greece. They came for the Olympic Festival, where they could watch top athletes compete for glory in sporting events and also worship at the sacred site of the Temple of Zeus.

The festival was filled with prayers, music, poetry, dance, great feasts and the sacrifice of a hundred oxen. It was at the height of summer, and for the spectators it was a break from their hard work after harvest – and a break from fighting wars with neighbouring city-states.

The festival conditions could be uncomfortable – you were scorched by the heat and crushed by the crowds, with swarms of flies buzzing around. But as the Greek poet Pindar (c.518–c.438 BCE) wrote,

'There is no festival more glorious than Olympia!'

A Legendary Beginning

Greek legends give different versions of how the Olympic Games began. Modern historians think they probably started as funeral games, to celebrate local dead heroes. One legend says they were set up by the great hero, Herakles, also known as Hercules, to honour his father.

Herakles had to complete twelve tasks called the Labours of Herakles. One of these was to clean out the massive stables of King Augeas of Elis in one single day. The stables hadn't been cleaned for over thirty years and they contained more than one thousand cattle that produced a vast quantity of dung.

To wash out the filth Herakles diverted the River Alpheios so that it flowed through the stables. When his task was over Herakles celebrated by making a clearing nearby in Olympia and setting up the Games there to honour his father, the god Zeus.

The ancient Greeks loved holding athletics festivals and the Olympic Games was one of four national festivals held regularly. Top athletes tried to win events in all four. All the athletics festivals, ranging from the big national events to small local ones, were held to honour a god or goddess.

The Glory of Zeus

A visit to the Olympic Festival was also a pilgrimage to the sanctuary of Olympia, a sacred grove known as the Altis.

A place of great religious importance to the ancient Greeks, the Altis became home to over seventy temples, statues and shrines, including the Temple of Zeus. Built in the 5th century BCE, it contained the huge statue of Zeus, which was considered to be one of the Seven Wonders of the Ancient World.

At 13 m high, visitors would have to stand far back to take in the statue's full glory. Glistening with gold and ivory, the statue showed Zeus on his throne, holding the winged goddess of victory, Nike, in his right hand and a golden sceptre topped with an eagle in his left.

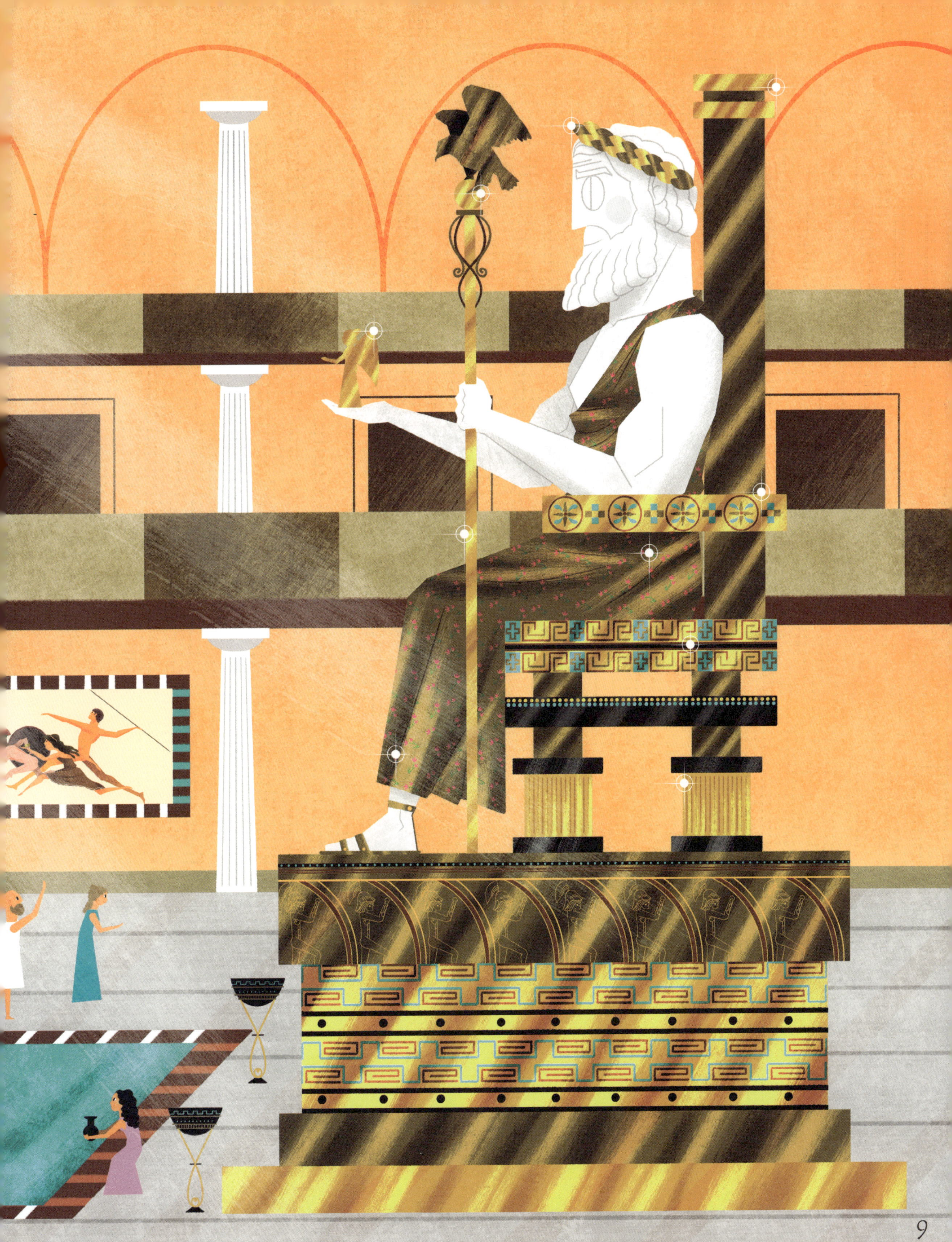

THE OLYMPIC SITE

The site of the Olympic Festival grew in size for each Olympic Games as temples, monuments and sports facilities were built around the sacred site. Over hundreds of years, these buildings were constantly improved or pulled down and rebuilt.

By 100 BCE the site featured a stadium for running, a *hippodrome* (horse track), a *palaistra* (exercise area), a bathhouse, swimming pool and gymnasium where athletes practised running and throwing events.

Training

Greek athletes took their training very seriously. They had to swear an oath saying that they had been training in their home towns for the previous ten months. At least a month before the Games began, the athletes travelled to the city of Elis to continue their preparations closer to Olympia.

There were three gymnasiums at Elis and the marketplace was turned into a practice race track for the chariot races. Athletes' lives were controlled by trainers who imposed strict diets and exercise plans. Any competitors who did not come up to scratch were disqualified before they even reached Olympia.

There was very little rest for the athletes before the Olympic festival. Two days before it began, the athletes, trainers, horses, chariots, officials and others formed a procession that followed a route known as the Sacred Way. They walked 58 km over the two days, the equivalent of walking a marathon on each day, to reach Olympia. Along the route, they stopped to perform religious ceremonies.

The Spectators and Judges

Spectators travelled to Olympia from across Greece and also from Greek settlements throughout southern Europe and the nearby coasts of Africa and Asia.

Only the top officials and important visitors had accommodation in the huge guesthouse called the *Leonidaion*, just outside the Altis. Everyone else slept in tents, or wrapped themselves in blankets and slept on the ground.

Rich or poor, there were no seats for spectators once the events began. Instead they crowded together on raised banks. There was a stand for the judges, the *hellanodikai* (this word means 'Judges of the Greeks' in ancient Greek), in the stadium with seats. They dressed in purple robes and were organisers as well as judges and also supervised the athletes' training in the month before the festival.

THE FIRST RACE

At the very first Olympic Games there was only one event – the *stade*, a 192-m sprint. According to myth, this distance was measured out by 600 of Herakles' footsteps.

The stadium did not exist and so the race was run on a level stretch of ground, with a line drawn in the sand marking the starting point. The first Olympic champion was a young cook from the city of Elis called Korebos. The *stade* was the most famous Olympic race and the whole Olympiad (the four years between each Olympic Games) was named after the winner of this race.

Later, the stadium had a marble start line formed of carved grooves for runners to grip with their toes. They began the race from a standing start, leaning slightly forward with their arms stretched outwards.

17

TRIASTES

Gradually, further events were added to the festival, with each Olympic Games attracting more spectators and more competitors eager to become an Olympic champion.

At the 14th Olympic Games, a second running event was added, the *diaulos*, which was a sprint of two lengths of the stadium. The 15th Olympic Games added the *dolichos*, a long-distance running race consisting of 20 or 24 lengths of the stadium. In these races the runners had to turn around posts at the far end and then return.

Occasionally, a brilliant athlete won all three running races. He was known as a *triastes*, or 'three-timer'. The greatest *triastes* of all was Leonidas of Rhodes, who won all three running races at three Olympics in a row between 164 and 152 BCE. The people of Rhodes were so proud of Leonidas that they worshipped him as a hero.

The Pentathlon

In 708 BCE the pentathlon was introduced. *Penta* means five in Greek and the pentathletes competed in five events: discus, long jump, javelin, running and wrestling, held in that order during one afternoon.

We are not sure how an athlete won. There was no points system, as we have in the pentathlon today. It seems that if an athlete won the first three events, he was declared the winner and the last two events were then cancelled.

By the time the pentathlon had been introduced, it's thought that the Greek athletes performed naked. No one is sure exactly why. One story tells of an Athenian runner who was about to win a race in 720 BCE when his shorts fell down and tripped him up! This may have led to the judges stating that all athletes had to perform naked so that this could not happen again.

21

The Discus

With a three-quarter twist of the body, the discus flew out of the athlete's grip, swirling out into the stadium grounds.

Each athlete had five throws, with an Olympic attendant marking its landing with a peg. Greek discuses were heavy, some weighing over 6 kg. They were made of bronze, lead or marble. The weight and throwing technique meant that the athletes could not throw the discuses as far as modern discus throwers.

Three official discuses were kept at Olympia, safely stored in a special treasury between Games to make the competition fair. Some discuses were made as religious offerings and had sacred messages around the rims.

THE LONG JUMP

Calming flute music filled the stadium as the pentathletes concentrated on the long jump. The music created a rhythm that helped with their timing as they prepared to jump and leap forward as far as they could.

The athletes carried *halteres,* large weights made of lead or stone, each weighing up to 4 kg. By swinging their arms, they used the weights to help them jump further.

From a standing start, the *halteres* were swung back and forth, with one mighty swing forwards for take-off. This helped propel the jumper forwards. As he came in to land, he swung them backwards, providing an extra forward thrust at the end. Historians are unsure whether the long jump was a single jump or a multiple jump, like the modern triple jump event.

The Javelin

Like many of the early Olympic events, learning to throw the javelin was part of a Greek soldier's training. Spears were also used for hunting.

The sporting javelins were lighter than those used as weapons and were made of elder wood, with a leather loop wound around the middle. The leather unwound as the javelin travelled through the air, making it spin. To launch the javelin, the athlete ran forwards to a mark on the ground, drew the javelin back in his right hand, extending his left hand to help with balance, and launched it forwards.

The best throws travelled more than 100 m. Although the athletes were all trained experts in javelin-throwing, there are accounts of people being speared accidentally during training.

27

Wrestling

Wrestling was part of the pentathlon and was also held as a separate event. The wrestlers entered the stadium to great cheers from the crowd. They were given nicknames based on how they looked, such as 'the bear' or 'the lion'.

Greek wrestlers were highly skilled but also vicious. Contestants were not allowed to bite their opponent or dig their fingers into their eyes or other soft bits of their body, but they were allowed to do almost anything else. Some wrestlers shaved their heads to avoid having their hair yanked. Like many Greek athletes, they oiled their bodies but then dusted them with powder to make them less slippery.

There were two types of wrestling match. In one, the aim was to throw an opponent to the ground three times. In the other, the wrestlers fought on until one of them surrendered. He did this by raising his right hand with his index finger pointing upwards.

29

Boxing

In 688 BCE, at the 23rd Olympiad, boxing was introduced. Greek boxers were tough. The fighters wore strips of leather tied around their hands which did not do much to soften the blows.

Boxing fights did not take place in a ring but in an open area. All sorts of blows were allowed although most boxers seem to have aimed for the head of their opponent.

One boxer, called Damoxenos, jabbed his opponent so hard under the ribs with his fingers that he pulled his guts out, killing him instantly. Normally a fight ended when one man surrendered, or passed out.

31

The Pankration

The *pankration*, a combination of boxing and wrestling, was the roughest sport of all.

The aim of the contest was to force your opponent to give up. Almost any tactics were allowed except for biting your opponent or gouging out their eyes. Some fighters ignored these rules but mostly they punched, wrestled, twisted their opponent's legs or arms or threw them to the ground.

Pankratiasts were famous for their strength and their methods. Sostratos of Sicyon was known for breaking his opponents' fingers, while the athlete known as 'Leaping Weight' twisted his opponents' feet out of their sockets. One of the most famous pankratiasts of all time was Polydamas of Skotussa who defeated all his opponents, including a lion.

RACE IN ARMOUR

The race in armour, or *hoplitodromos*, was the last race of the Games. Named after the foot soldiers, the hoplites, it was a perfect sport for military training.

Wearing helmets and greaves (armour for the lower leg) and carrying shields, twenty-five athletes ran down the stadium to the shouts of the crowd. The runners had to run around the post at the end of the stadium, a tight corner made more difficult by having to carry the large shields.

Running with the weight of the shield and armour made this a test of strength as well as speed. Sometimes, the athletes dropped their shields or collided with each other.

CHARIOT RACES

Packed into the *hippodrome*, for many spectators the chariot races were the most exciting part of the Olympic Games.

At the sound of the trumpet, teams of horses sped off pulling chariots driven by charioteers. The chariot wheels threw up clouds of dust as the charioteers overtook opponents, took tight corners and sometimes overturned in spectacular crashes.

There were two types of chariot race, one using a team of two horses and the other using a team of four. There were separate contests for teams of young horses, called colts, and for horses of any age. The races varied in length from about 4 km to over 12 km.

The chariots were made of wood, painted wickerwork and strips of leather. The charioteers did not usually own the chariots or horses but were employed by wealthy owners, who took all the glory if they won.

HERALDS AND TRUMPETERS

At the 96th Olympic Games held in 396 BCE, a different sort of competition was introduced to find the best heralds and trumpeters.

Running up to an Olympic Games, three heralds travelled across the Greek world, telling people the date of the next Olympic Games, inviting them to attend and giving details of the Olympic Truce.

At the Games, the heralds announced the beginning of each event while the trumpeters played before the winners' names were read out.

The heralds' and trumpeters' competition was held in the morning of the first day of the festival, and the prize was the honour of announcing the forthcoming events and winners.

The contest took place at the end of the Echo Colonnade, a long narrow building that was between the *hippodrome* and the stadium. Its design meant that a man's voice could echo there seven times or more. The judges were looking for the trumpeter who produced the clearest, loudest sound.

THE WOMEN'S GAMES

Women were not allowed to compete in the Olympics, although they were allowed to enter their horses and chariots. However, they did have their own sporting festival called the Heraia.

From around the 6th century BCE, the Heraia was held every four years at Olympia in honour of the goddess Hera. The officials and organisers were all women and the competitors were unmarried women from across Greece. Athletes competed in sprint races in the stadium, divided into three races according to the age of the competitors. They ran shorter distances than the men.

Unlike the men, women athletes did not compete naked but wore a short dress hung from one shoulder. The winners were crowned with wreaths of olive branches and given a share of a cow sacrificed to Hera. Other women's games were held across Greece.

Hail the Champions

At the ancient Olympics, no one cared who came second or third. Only the winner was important.

Winning at the Olympics was every athlete's dream, bringing great honour and glory. The winners were crowned with an olive wreath, woven from branches cut from a sacred olive tree growing in the Altis. They were also presented with a palm branch and had pieces of wool tied to parts of their body to show they were the champions.

A winning athlete's fame lived on after the Games. If the athlete was wealthy, or his friends and family had the money, they paid for a statue of him to be erected in the Altis. Back home, feasts were held to welcome returning champions. They were often given money, good jobs and even free food for life.

The Olympic Legacy

The Olympic Games took place until CE 393, even after Greece came under the control of the Roman Empire. As Christianity became the religion of the Romans, laws banned the worship of all but the Christian god. The days of Zeus and his Olympic Games were over.

Remains of the old site in Olympia can be seen today, such as these temple columns.

Slowly, the buildings at Olympia fell into ruin due to fire, earthquakes, storms and floods. All that was left lay buried under a layer of silt until an Englishman, Richard Chandler, rediscovered the site in 1766.

Archaeologists started careful excavations of the site a hundred years later, funded by the German government. Their finds helped inspire the idea of staging the Olympic Games again. In 1894, the International Olympic Committee was set up to plan the first modern Olympic Games, held in Athens, Greece in 1896.

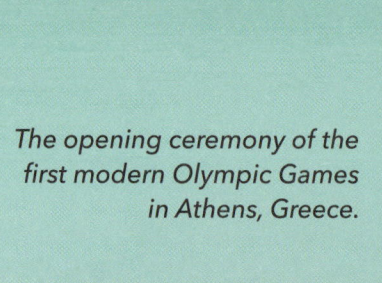

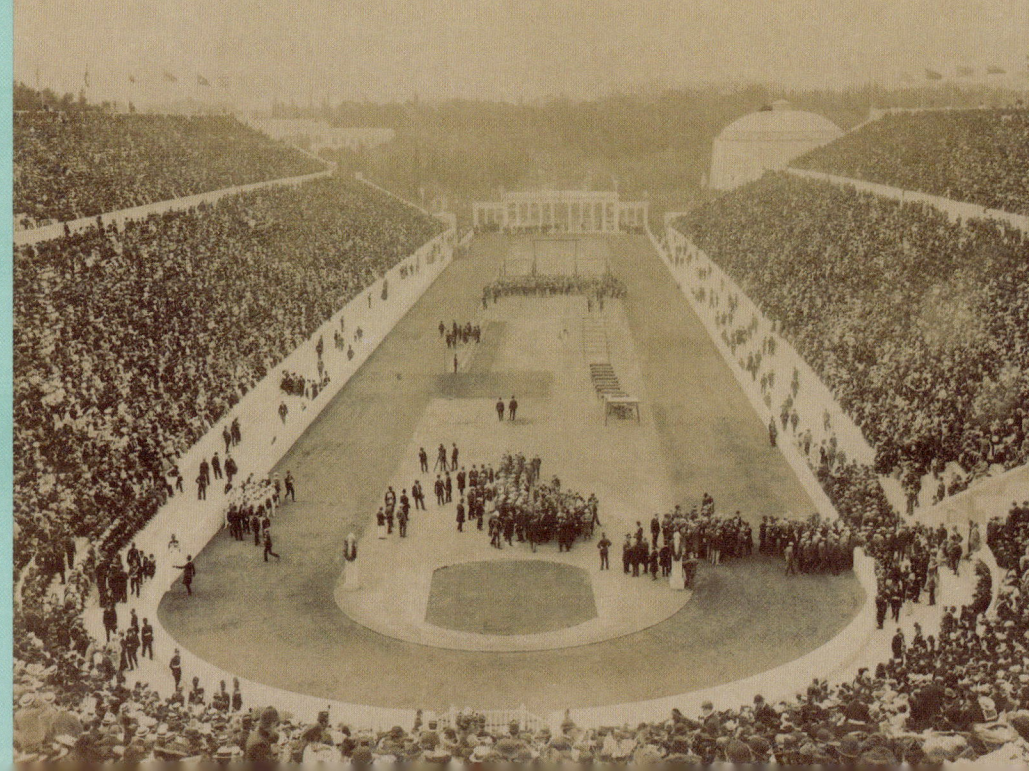

The opening ceremony of the first modern Olympic Games in Athens, Greece.

The 1896 Games saw the introduction of new sports, such as the shot put.

The Games continue to create sporting heroes, such as Usain Bolt, seen here competing in the 2016 Rio Olympics.

The opening ceremony of the 2016 Rio Olympics, the 31st modern Olympic Games, where 207 nations took part.

The modern Olympics have survived to this day and, just as in ancient Greece, an Olympic victory is every athlete's highest goal. People from every corner of the globe come together to compete in the modern Olympic Games. The Games remain one of the ancient Greeks' finest legacies to the modern world.

Further Information

The Modern Games

In 1896, the first modern Olympic Games took place. It was the Frenchman Baron Pierre de Coubertin who worked with a group of people to organise these first modern Games, held in Athens, Greece. Only 14 countries took part but the Games were a great success.

Since then, the Olympic Games have been held every four years, except for during the First and Second World Wars. Each modern Olympics is held in a different city around the world and they have become huge events. Running races and other track and field events still take place alongside sports that the ancient Greeks would not recognise, such as cycling and football. There are Winter and Summer Olympic Games, as well as the Paralympics for disabled athletes. Just as the ancient Olympics brought the people of ancient Greece together in peace, one of the aims of the modern Olympics is to spread peace and understanding between countries.

Resources

Books:
The Olympics: Ancient and Modern by Joe Fullman (Wayland, 2017)

The Sports Timeline Wallbook by Christopher Lloyd (What on Earth Publishing, 2019)

The Unofficial Guide to Olympic Champions by Paul Mason (Wayland, 2019)

The Unofficial Guide to Olympic Events by Paul Mason (Wayland, 2019)

Websites:
www.bbc.com/bitesize/articles/z36j7ty

www.britishmuseum.org/learn/schools/ages-7-11/ancient-greece/classroom-resource-olympic-games

www.olympic.org/ancient-olympic-games

www.penn.museum/sites/olympics/olympicorigins.shtml

The website addresses (URLSs) included in this book were valid at the time of going to press. However, it is possible that contents or addresses may have changed since the publication of this book. No responsibility for any such changes can be accepted by the publisher.

Glossary

bathhouse A public building with hot, cold and warm baths as well as a steam room.

Christianity The religion based on the teachings of Jesus Christ and the belief that he was the son of God.

city-state In ancient Greece, a city and the land around it, with its own government, laws and army.

excavation When archaeologists carefully dig down, removing soil, to find any buried remains of people, objects or buildings.

gouge an eye Press very hard on someone's eye, which could result in injury or even blindness.

grove A small group of trees.

gymnasium A training area, or building, where Greek men and boys took exercise or improved their sporting skills.

herald A person whose job it is to announce messages, often gaining people's attention by blowing a trumpet.

hippodrome The track on which horse races took place.

legend A story from ancient times about people and events that may, or may not, have happened.

oath A promise to do something. At the ancient Olympic Games, the oath was to follow the rules, which athletes promised to do in front of the statue of Zeus.

olive wreath Branches of an olive tree woven into a circle to fit a person's head.

Olympic Truce The period of peace, when any wars should be stopped to allow people to travel to and from, or compete in, the Olympic Games.

opponent A person that you are racing against, fighting against or in a contest with.

pilgrimage A journey to a holy place.

sacred Connected to a god or goddess.

sacrifice Animals were sacrificed, or killed, at the ancient Olympic Games, and offered as gifts to the gods and goddesses.

Seven Wonders of the Ancient World The seven greatest places of the ancient world, as listed by Philo of Byzantium in 225 BCE. The list included the statue of Zeus at Olympia, the lighthouse of Alexandria and the Great Pyramid at Giza.

silt Fine grains of sand and mud, carried in river water.

spectator Someone who is watching an event.

stadium A large building for open-air sport.

tactics The skills or planned actions used to achieve something.

temple A place of worship.

treasury A place where valuable objects, or money, are stored.

wickerwork Objects made by twisting and weaving thin lengths of wood together.

Zeus King of the ancient Greek gods.

Index

accommodation 15
Altis 8, 15, 42–43
archaeologists 44

boxing 30–32

chariots 12–13, 36–37, 40
Christianity 44
Coubertin, Baron de 46

Damoxenos 31
diaulos 18
dolichos 18
discus 20, 22–23

Echo Colonnade 39
Elis 6, 12, 16

feasts 4, 43
funeral games 6

gymnasiums 11–12

Hera 40–41
Heraia 40–41
Herakles 6–7, 16
heralds 38–39
hippodrome 11, 36, 39
hoplites 34
hoplitodromos 34

International Olympic Committee 44

javelin 20, 26–27
judges 14–15, 20, 39

King Augeas of Elis 6
Korebos 16

Leonidaion 15
Leonidas of Rhodes 19

long jump 20, 24–25

music 4, 24, 38–39

oath, Olympic 12
Olympic Games, modern 44–46
Olympic Truce 38

palaistra 11
pankration 32–33
Paralympics 46
pentathlon 20–29
Pindar 5
Polydamas of Skotussa 33

race in armour 34–35
races, chariot 12, 36–37
races, running 11, 16–20, 34–35, 40, 45–46
Roman Empire 44

Sacred Way 13
soldiers, Greek 26, 34
Sostratos of Sicyon 33
spectators 4, 14–15, 18, 36
stade 16–17
stadium 11, 15–18, 22, 24, 28, 34, 39, 40

Temple of Zeus 4, 8–9
temples 4, 8–10
training 11–13, 15, 26
triastes 18–19
trumpeters 36, 38–39

women 40–41
wreaths, olive 41–42
wrestling 20, 28–29, 32–33

Zeus 4, 6–9, 44